United States
Department of
Agriculture

Forest Service

Pacific Northwest
Research Station

General Technical
Report
PNW-GTR-826
July 2010

Wood Energy for Residential Heating in Alaska: Current Conditions, Attitudes, and Expected Use

David L. Nicholls, Allen M. Brackley, and Valerie Barber

Authors

David L. Nicholls is a forest products technologist and **Allen M. Brackley** is a research forester, Alaska Wood Utilization Research and Development Center, 204 Siginaka Way, Sitka, AK 99835; and **Valerie Barber** is an assistant professor, Forest Products Program, University of Alaska-Fairbanks, 533 E Fireweed Ave., Palmer, AK 99645.

Cover photographs: cordwood by David Nicholls; stoves by Allen Brackley.

Abstract

Nicholls, David L.; Brackley, Allen M.; Barber, Valerie. 2010. Wood energy
for residential heating in Alaska: current conditions, attitudes, and expected
use. Gen. Tech. Rep. PNW-GTR-826. Portland, OR: U.S. Department of
Agriculture, Forest Service, Pacific Northwest Research Station. 30 p.

This study considered three aspects of residential wood energy use in Alaska:
current conditions and fuel consumption, knowledge and attitudes, and future use
and conditions. We found that heating oil was the primary fuel for home heating
in southeast and interior Alaska, whereas natural gas was used most often in
south-central Alaska (Anchorage). Firewood heating played a much more important role as a secondary (vs. primary) heating source in all regions of Alaska. In
interior Alaska, there was a somewhat greater interest in the use of wood energy
compared to other regions. Likewise, consumption of fossil fuels was considerably greater in interior Alaska. Cost was a primary factor influencing motivation
to convert to wood energy. Most respondents were at least somewhat familiar
with residential wood-burning systems, however relatively few were familiar with
Environmental Protection Agency certified woodstoves. Firewood/cordwood
was by far the preferred wood fuel choice, whereas wood briquettes were least
preferred. Similarly, firewood was the type of wood fuel that respondents were
most familiar with. Variations were observed between Alaska's primary regions
(southeast, south-central, and interior). This could be attributed to a number of
factors including colder climates in interior Alaska, and overall low use of wood
energy in south-central Alaska because of preferences for natural gas. Fuel oil
prices of $4.00 to $5.00 per gallon would be needed for most homeowners to
convert to wood heating. There was a broad range of willingness to pay for new
wood energy systems (from about $1,000 to $3,000). However, this survey was
not random and results may not be representative of the populations at each
sampling location.

Keywords: Alaska, biomass, bioenergy, wood energy, renewable, cordwood,
pellets, fossil fuels.

Introduction

Given the peak in fuel oil prices during 2008, there has been an increased interest in renewable energy for home heating in many areas in Alaska. Wood energy is an important renewable energy option in forested regions of the state, and can be easily implemented on a small scale using local resources. During the past few years, a resurgence of wood energy for home heating has occurred in addition to larger scale wood heating facilities, including a school (Craig, Alaska) and several wood products facilities having lumber dry kilns (Craig, Thorne Bay, Hoonah, and Delta Junction, Alaska). On Prince of Wales Island, feasibility assessments have identified potential opportunities for even more facilities, including cordwood heating of schools, community centers, and several other public buildings (T.R. Miles 2006). In Sitka, a city resolution has set a goal of using "local labor and materials including recycled paper and cardboard" to heat 800 homes by the end of 2009 (City and Borough of Sitka, Alaska 2008). Benefits of increased use of biomass energy in Alaska could include reduced home heating costs, efficient use of waste products, and additional revenues for local sawmills. Other benefits that could be more difficult to quantify include carbon emission reductions, improved forest health, and habitat and watershed restoration benefits (Tongass Futures Roundtable 2008).

Natural gas is the major fuel used in south-central Alaska. There have been recent price increases for this source of energy, and the potential exists for natural gas shortages in this region by 2012, especially if colder than normal winters persist (Loy 2009). Regardless of these factors, natural gas still has a competitive advantage over wood in south-central Alaska, although with an uncertain future. In interior Alaska, heating oil is commonly used for residential heating. However, wood energy is being increasingly used for residential heating, and larger facilities have been established in Delta Junction and Dot Lake, Alaska (Nicholls 2009). Although high fuel oil prices have resulted in a significant interest in wood energy, recent price fluctuations underscore the importance of developing stable fuel sources not subject to demand based on world markets or changing economic conditions.

An important first step in adopting wood energy will be understanding consumer preferences for various wood energy products, the types of existing and new equipment, and the ones preferred by residential consumers. Several wood energy equipment dealers in southeast Alaska have become established, and in recent years business has increased considerably (Bauman 2005). Other forest products firms and fuel suppliers have expanded their product lines to include firewood. Fuel availability differs by region, but wood energy products that are available to southeast Alaska residents include firewood/cordwood (figs. 1 and 2), pellets (fig. 3), and other densified fuel products. Cordwood is firewood cut and split into conveniently

An important first step in adopting wood energy will be understanding consumer preferences for various wood energy products, the types of existing and new equipment, and the ones preferred by residential consumers.

Figure 1—Firewood bundles for sale at a grocery store in southeast Alaska.

Figure 2—Stacked cordwood at a wood-burning facility in south-central Alaska.

David Nicholls

Figure 3–Wood pellets for sale at a grocery store in southeast Alaska.

sized pieces for easy stacking. Pellets are made from compacted sawdust or other wood waste products. Biobricks are made from compressed wood waste (like pellets) but formed into larger stackable bricks. On Prince of Wales Island, a new biomass cooperative has been formed among local mill owners to combine and utilize mill waste wood. A business plan is being developed to build a facility to manufacture biobricks for an alternative source of energy.

In 2007, the Fairbanks Economic Development Council conducted a survey to determine interest of consumers in the Fairbanks area to convert to wood pellets (Robb 2007). When consumers were made aware of the costs, 42 percent of those in the southeast and 55 percent of those in the Fairbanks areas stated they would consider converting to pellet fuel. Important wood fuel properties include unit size, density, moisture content, and moisture resistance. Also important will be fuel delivery method and labor requirements to prepare, transport, and burn fuel in homes. In Sitka and other parts of southeast Alaska having limited road systems, an important consideration will be whether wood fuel is to be transported by barge from outlying areas (vs. harvested adjacent to local roads). Already, a major wood products facility in southeast Alaska is producing firewood and has started delivery service to regional markets by barge.

Challenges to increased wood energy use in Alaska include having relatively few wood products producers or harvesters capable of supplying firewood on a steady basis and in economic quantities. Once the extent of wood fuel markets is known, interested entrepreneurs can plan business startup activities for production and distribution of wood fuel as well as sales of wood-burning equipment.

Potential Wood Fuel Sources

The following sections identify potential sources of wood fuel, and these could differ by region. For example, more sawmill residues could be available for wood energy in southeast Alaska, whereas in south-central and interior Alaska, other sources, such as hazardous fuel clearings, could be used.

Sawmill Residues

There is limited information relative to the volume of lumber produced in Alaska outside the southeast region. Southeast Alaska is home to 12 active mills, 3 of which each produce in excess of 3 million board feet annually. Since 2002, actual lumber production in southeast Alaska has ranged between 31 and 34.6 million board feet per year (Brackley and Crone 2009, Brackley et al. 2006). About half of the stated log volume is processed into lumber, and the remaining volume includes slabs, edging, chips, sawdust, bark, and trim ends. Sawmill residuals are located at the mill site, in proximity to users, and available for use or conversion to various energy products.

Harvesting Residues

Saw logs are the only product harvested by most logging operations in Alaska. In all areas of Alaska, trees and portions of trees that are not suitable for saw logs can be recovered and processed into energy products. The potential sources of energy products include rough and rotten trees, tops, limbs, and stems from trees that are below the size required to produce saw logs. In all harvesting operations, a transportation system has been established to move material from stump to market. A case-by-case analysis of the economics of producing energy products from existing harvest areas is beyond the scope of this paper. Obviously, harvesting areas that are near users have a higher potential than those in remote areas.

Thinnings From Forest Management Activities

Approximately 425,000 acres of the Tongass National Forest in southeast Alaska have been harvested since 1950 (Nowacki et al. 2001). Option 6 of the Tongass Land Management Plan (USDA FS 2008) identifies 225,000 acres available for future thinning. Thinnings have the potential to provide both high-value products such as house logs and biomass for home and district heating projects. Wildlife habitat enhancement on Prince of Wales Island includes a variety of silvicultural operations such as precommercial thinning, commercial thinning, pruning, gap creation, and tree planting (USDA FS 2007). During fiscal years 2004 through 2007, an average of 5,449 acres per year were precommercially thinned in the Tongass National Forest.[1] During fall 2007 in a managed watershed near Sitka (Starrigavan area), forest restoration activities treated 10 acres. This stand was about 35 years old and yielded close to 18 cords of firewood to 31 clients.[2] Although each client used only about half a cord of firewood, this could provide significant benefits to residents who use wood as a secondary heating source.

DeMars (2000) found that precommercial thinning of spruce-hemlock (*Picea sitchensis* (Bong.) Carr. and *Tsuga heterophylla* (Raf.) Sarg.) stands in southeast Alaska were generally beneficial when managing for wood production, and that medium to heavy thinnings should be favored. Heavy thinning could reduce wood quality; however, wildlife habitat could be improved through additional understory vegetation. Other studies considered Sitka spruce and western hemlock management on high-productivity and low-productivity sites in southeast Alaska (Barbour et al. 2005). By using the forest vegetation simulator (FVS), researchers found that precommercial thinnings could be used at stand age 20, and that stand spacing (ranging from 12.1 ft by 12.1 ft to 20 ft by 20 ft) had an important influence on merchantable timber volume.

Hazardous Fuel Clearings

Some communities in Alaska are close to hazardous fuels that increase fire risk. For example, in the Fairbanks area, 250 acres has already been harvested in the Cash Creek drainage to reduce hazardous fuel loads. It is estimated that over 100,000 green tons of biomass could become available for power generation in the Fairbanks area within the next 10 years (assuming harvests on 5,000 total acres of 20 green tons per acre) (Nicholls et al. 2006). More than 1,200 acres are listed within 13 hazardous fuel treatment units in the Fairbanks area (Hanson 2007), potentially offering additional opportunities for biomass utilization. One of the potential problems with using hazardous fuel removals for bioenergy is the possibility of a sudden surge of biomass over a short timeframe as severe fire risks

---

[1] Spores, S. 2008. Personal communication. Acting forest silviculturist, Tongass National Forest, 648 Mission St., Ketchikan, AK 99901.

[2] Heuer, P. 2008. Personal communication. Silviculturist, Tongass National Forest, 204 Siginaka Way, Sitka, AK 99835.

are being mitigated, and conversely, potential shortfalls in biomass supply during years in which few acres burn.

Research Objectives

A specific objective of this study is to characterize the current use of wood energy for residential heating in Alaska's three most populated regions.

This study evaluates wood energy use by residential consumers in Alaska (fig. 4). The scope of this project is to evaluate current consumer knowledge and attitudes in Alaska relative to wood energy use versus other heating fuels. A specific objective of this study is to characterize the current use of wood energy for residential heating in Alaska's three most populated regions (southeast, south-central, and interior). The scope of this paper is to evaluate conditions related to future and expected conditions for residential wood energy use in Alaska. Specific objectives include:

- Assess heating oil prices needed to induce Alaska residents to convert to wood energy.
- Evaluate daily maintenance time that wood energy adopters would be willing to spend.
- Evaluate willingness to pay for new wood energy systems and for home energy efficiency measures.

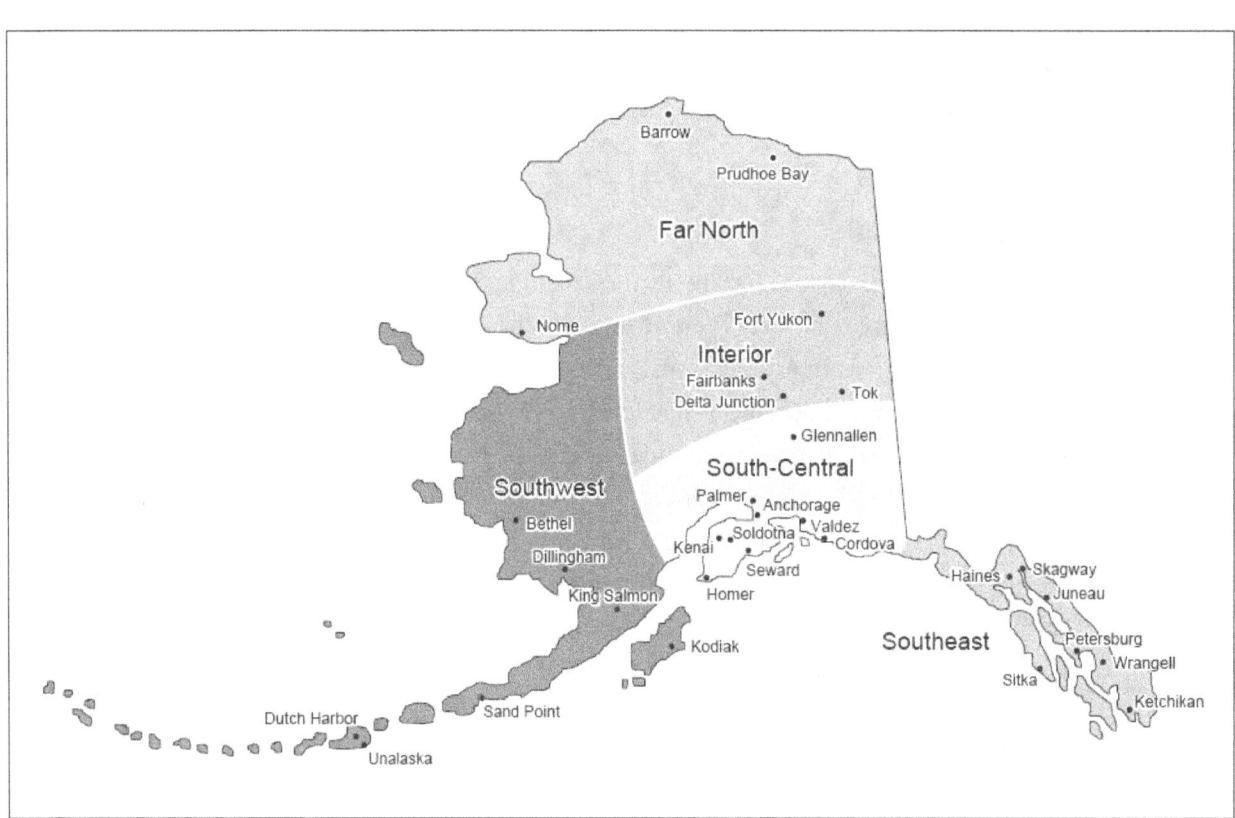

Figure 4—State of Alaska, indicating regions.

Methods

In this study, we evaluated consumer preferences for renewable energy by using survey methods. The survey was conducted at local businesses in five Alaska locations (tables 1 and 2). Venues included hardware stores and home improvement centers, grocery stores, a large "big-box" retail center, and a home and garden show. Most locations were sampled over several days (however, two of the locations in Fairbanks were sampled for only 1 day). All surveys were conducted in partnership with the University of Alaska-Fairbanks (UAF), Cooperative State Research, Education, and Extension Service, Forest Products Program. Surveys were reviewed and approved for use by the UAF Institutional Review Board.

Table 1—Wood energy survey sampling locations for five communities in Alaska

| Location | Sampling dates | Sampling venue | | | | |
		Home center	Grocery store	Hardware store	Home show	"Big box" store
Sitka	March–May 2008	X	X	X		
Juneau	May 2008		X	X		
Ketchikan	September 2008			X		X
Anchorage	September 2008				X	
Fairbanks	September 2008	X		X		

Table 2—Regional response rate to Alaska wood energy use survey

Region	Sample locations	Number of usable responses	Percentage of total
			Percent
Southeast	Sitka, Juneau, Ketchikan	477	62.9
South-central	Anchorage, Matanuska-Susitna Valley	141	18.6
Interior	Fairbanks and outlying communities	140	18.5
Total		758	100.0

Response data were collected in Sitka (March–May 2008), in Juneau (May 2008), and in Anchorage, Ketchikan, and Fairbanks (September 2008). Note that home heating oil prices in general experienced a significant increase during our sampling period (March to September 2008). Thus, survey results may have differed if a respondent had answered in September versus in March. The surveys considered preferences for renewable energy use, equipment, and energy products. A total of 758 usable responses were collected (from the 509 participants in southeast, 149 in south-central, and 146 in interior Alaska). Screening questions were used so that a respondent who was under 18 years old, from a household that had already responded, or not a local resident, was omitted from the survey results.

Respondents were asked to consider only space heating applications for their home. Because several of the questions pertained to household energy use, we evaluated only one survey per household. Respondents who were landlords were asked to provide information based on all properties owned (e.g., total use of energy for home heating). Those who were renters were still permitted to complete surveys, although people whose primary residence was a boat were not included. No information on household income was collected. Surveys were conducted at various times of the day and various days of the week (including weekdays and weekends). Prospective respondents were asked at random if they would be interested in completing a survey; however, there was no way to control who actually completed surveys (and so the survey was not random).[3] Thus, the survey was not representative of each region or location sampled. For example, the state's largest population center, Anchorage, was sampled at only one location (a home show), whereas in southeast Alaska, samples were conducted at seven locations in three cities. Also, we conducted the survey in urban areas (the largest Alaskan cities), and there are likely differences in viewpoints between these residents and those living in rural towns and villages.

Questions were broadly grouped into three themes, all relating to use of wood energy for home heating (complete survey is provided in the appendix):

- Current conditions for household wood energy use
- Knowledge and attitudes of residential energy consumers
- Future (expected) use of wood energy

Visual displays of firewood, pellets, and densified wood fuel were present while respondents completed their surveys. An incentive (small candy or key chain) was also offered to respondents who completed a survey.

Results

This paper focuses on current conditions for residential heating with wood energy in Alaska, including primary and secondary home heating sources as well as fossil fuel type, price, and consumption. The data were evaluated based on geographic region (southeast, south-central, interior) and by gender (male vs. female respondents).

---

[3] It was observed that people who seemed more interested in wood energy were more likely to take the time to complete a survey.

Primary Home Heating Source

This survey found that heating oil was the primary fuel for home heating in southeast and interior Alaska, whereas natural gas dominated in south-central Alaska (including Anchorage) (fig. 5). Heating sources were more diversified in southeast Alaska, where electricity and firewood also played important roles. Very few respondents (less than 1 percent of responses, statewide) indicated using wood pellets as a primary heating source (fig. 5). Firewood use (cords per year) was moderately higher in the interior region vs. other regions.

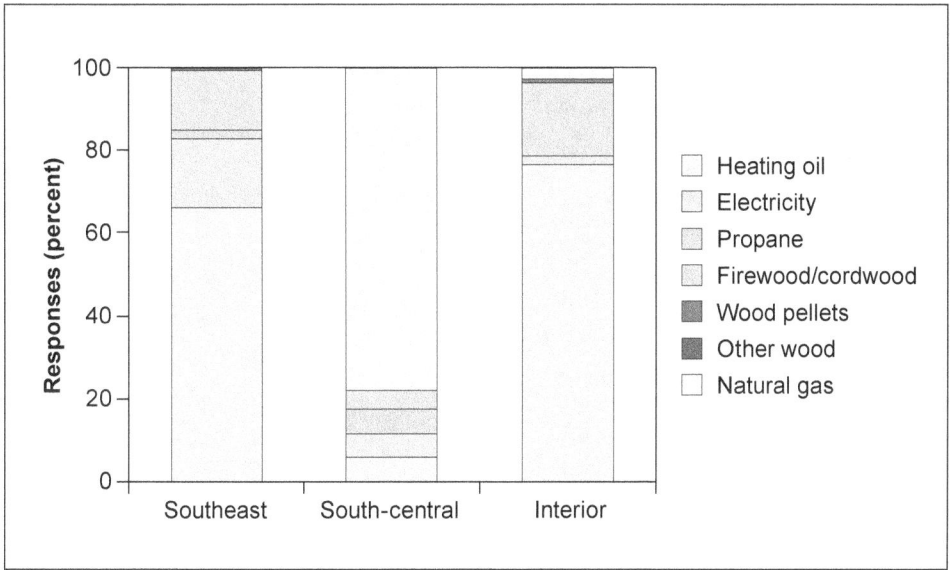

Figure 5—Primary fuel used for home heating, by Alaska region.

Secondary Home Heating Source

In general, secondary home heating represented a much more diverse energy mix (vs. primary heating) (table 3). Firewood heating played a much more important role, especially in south-central and interior Alaska, where it was the leading secondary home heating energy source. In most cases, electricity was preferred to heating oil for secondary heating, and this was especially true in southeast Alaska.

Firewood heating played an important role, especially in south-central and interior Alaska.

Wood Heating Use and Equipment Purchases

Most respondents had considered wood as a home heating source, with the greatest interest occurring in the interior region (for both male and female respondents) (table 4). Of those using wood fuel, firewood was preferred by a wide margin over wood pellets (table 5). Average firewood use was greatest in the interior region

Table 3—Secondary home heating source for respondents, by Alaska region

Region	Heating source	Number of responses	Percentage of regional total
			Percent
Southeast	Heating oil	73	22.7
	Electricity	156	48.4
	Propane	15	4.7
	Firewood/cordwood	74	23.0
	Wood pellets	4	1.2
	Natural gas	0	0
	Regional total	322	100
South-central	Heating oil	2	2.5
	Electricity	26	32.1
	Propane	4	4.9
	Firewood/cordwood	48	59.3
	Wood pellets	0	0
	Natural gas	1	1.2
	Regional total	81	100
Interior	Heating oil	17	18.5
	Electricity	16	17.4
	Propane	1	1.1
	Firewood/cordwood	56	60.8
	Wood pellets	2	2.2
	Natural gas	0	0
	Regional total	92	100

Table 4—Wood heating interest and equipment purchases

		Have you considered wood as a home heating source?				Have you purchased any wood-burning equipment within the past 10 years?			
		Male		Female		Male		Female	
Alaska region		Number of responses	Percentage of total	Number of responses	Percentage of total	Number of responses	Percentage of total	Number of responses	Percentage of total
			Percent		*Percent*		*Percent*		*Percent*
Southeast	Yes	210	74	100	69	77	28	31	22
	No	75	26	45	31	203	73	113	78
	Total	285	100	145	100	280	100	144	100
South-central	Yes	44	70	36	49	17	27	16	22
	No	19	30	38	51	45	73	57	78
	Total	63	100	74	100	62	100	73	100
Interior	Yes	93	83	20	80	51	46	8	33
	No	19	17	5	20	59	54	16	67
	Total	112	100	25	100	110	100	24	100

Table 5—Firewood and wood pellet consumption for home heating, based on respondents who indicated some use of wood fuel

Alaska region	Firewood consumption		Wood pellet consumption	
	Average cords per year	Number of responses	Average tons per year	Number of responses
	Cords		*Tons*	
Southeast	3.61	135	2.65	5
South-central	2.32	38	0	0
Interior	4.43	63	3.33	3

(versus other regions) for both male and female respondents. Firewood use in south-central Alaska was the lowest of any region, based on number of responses and also average cords per year.

Fewer respondents had actually purchased wood heating systems within the past 10 years (and again, the greatest interest in wood heating was by interior Alaska respondents). In the 2000 Census (U.S. Census Bureau 2000), it was estimated that wood was the primary fuel for home heating in about 4 percent of Alaska households (fig. 6). The Census does not collect any information about secondary sources of energy for home heating. Our survey data indicated a considerably higher use of wood fuel (approximately 30 percent of total respondents). However, our survey included primary and secondary heating use, and did not cover all regions of Alaska (but rather focused on the largest cities in Alaska). Furthermore, the survey was not random in that people having a greater interest in wood may have been more likely to voluntarily complete a survey, and the survey was generally offered only for a short period at each sampling location. Lastly, the season could have influenced respondent attitudes and answers. For example, the Fairbanks survey was administered during late September (beginning of the winter heating season), whereas in Sitka, responses were collected in spring (end of heating season).

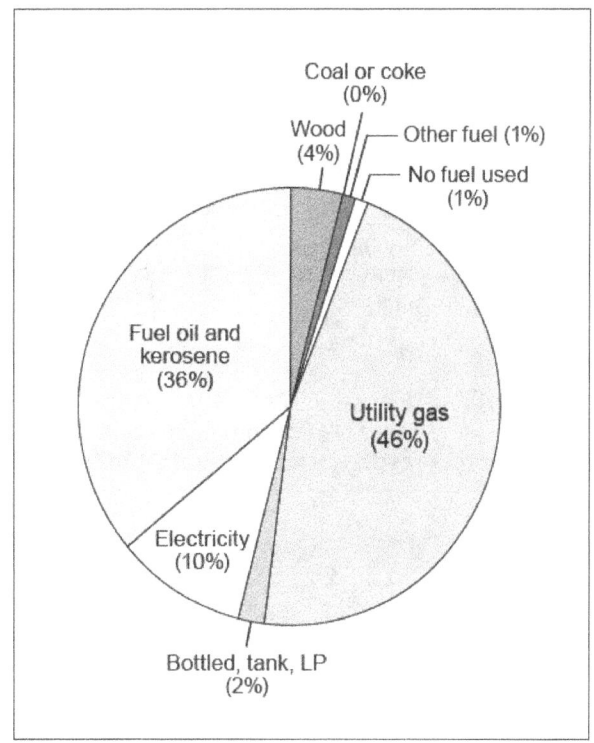

Figure 6—Primary fuel used for home heating in Alaska (source: U.S. Census Bureau 2000).

Fossil Fuel Type, Price, and Consumption

In our survey, fuel oil was the most widely used fossil fuel (table 6); however, most natural gas use occurred in the south-central region. Consumption of fossil fuel (among those who indicated some use of fossil fuels) was considerably greater in interior Alaska vs. southeast or south-central Alaska (table 7). Fuel oil prices were relatively uniform across the state (ranging from about $4.10 to $4.25 per gallon) (table 8). It should be noted that prices have fallen considerably since the data were collected (during spring, summer, and fall of 2008), and the time this report was prepared (December 2009).

Table 6—Fossil fuel type used for residential heating in Alaska, based on respondents who indicated some use of fossil fuels

Fossil fuel type	Number of responses	Percentage of total
		Percent
Fuel oil[a]	439	75.9
Natural gas	113	19.6
Propane	17	2.9
Kerosene	9	1.6
Total	578	100

[a] Includes No. 1 heating oil, No. 2 heating oil, No. 1 diesel, and No. 2 diesel.

Table 7—Fossil fuel[a] consumption for residential heating in Alaska, based on respondents who indicated some use of fossil fuels

Alaska region	Number of responses	Percentage of total regional responses	Average household fossil fuel consumption
		Percent	*Gallons per year*
Southeast	178	37	749.2
South-central	6	4	750.0
Interior	81	58	1,151.5

[a] Includes No. 1 heating oil, No. 2 heating oil, No. 1 diesel, No. 2 diesel, kerosene, and propane.

Table 8—Fossil fuel[a] price for residential heating in Alaska, based on respondents who indicated some use of fossil fuels

Alaska region	Number of responses	Percentage of total regional responses	Average fossil fuel price
		Percent	*Dollars per gallon*
Southeast	214	45	4.21
South-central	8	6	4.24
Interior	86	61	4.09

[a] Includes No. 1 heating oil, No. 2 heating oil, No. 1 diesel, No. 2 diesel, kerosene, and propane.

Factors to Motivate Conversion to Wood Energy

Cost was the key factor influencing respondent's motivation to convert to wood energy from some other fuel type (see fig. 7). Interior Alaska respondents were especially cost-conscious, whereas southeast Alaska respondents were less concerned about overall cost. In general, respondents were not concerned about a lack of local wood energy equipment vendors, and this was especially true in the interior region (Fairbanks). Of the three regions sampled, southeast Alaska respondents were the most concerned about finding local equipment vendors or local wood fuel suppliers.

Cost was the key factor influencing respondent's motivation to convert to wood energy.

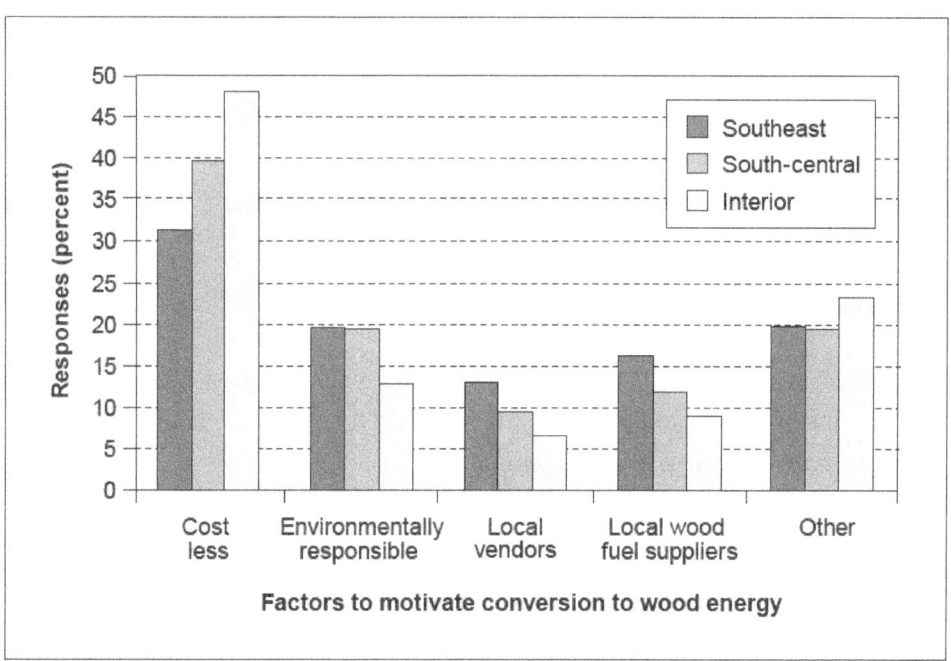

Figure 7—Factors to motivate conversion to wood energy, by Alaska region.

Potential Barriers to Wood Energy Use

Here, respondents were provided with a list of potential barriers (i.e., negative attributes) that could either prevent them from converting to future use of wood energy or might restrict their current use of wood energy. Note that within the "other" category, a number of positive comments were voluntarily offered (see fig. 8). The written comments by those who selected "other" included a variety of other barriers, such as fire hazard, lack of storage room for wood fuel, high initial/conversion expenses, asthma, allergies, and environmental concerns. The fact that so many written comments were offered (197 total) suggests that wood energy is very much on people's "radar."

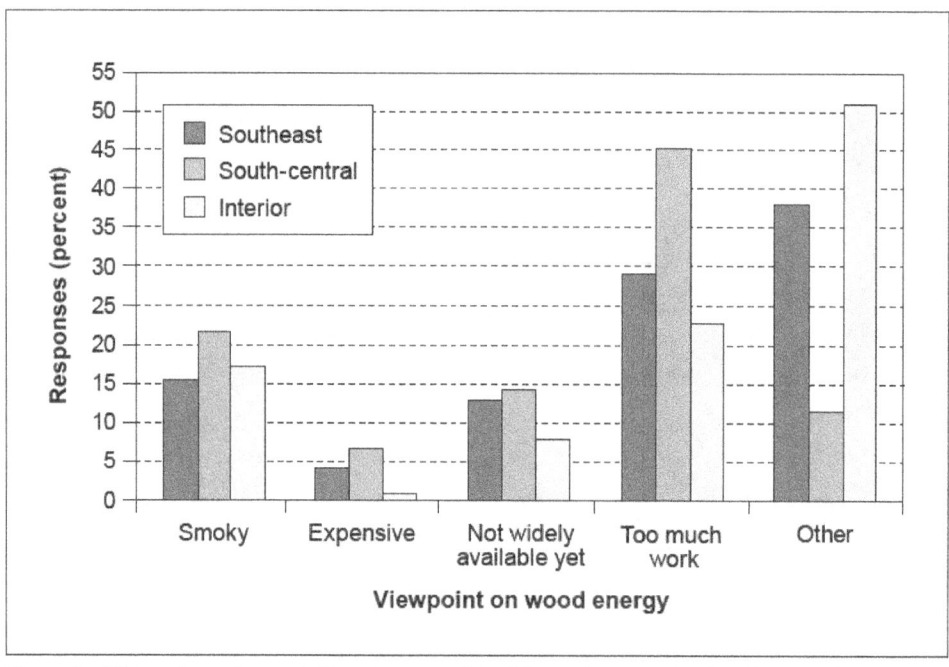

Figure 8—Viewpoint and potential barriers to residential wood energy use, by Alaska region. Note: The written comments by those who selected "other" included a variety of other barriers, such as fire hazard, lack of storage room for wood fuel, high initial/conversion expenses, asthma, allergies, and environmental concerns.

"Too much work" was the main barrier or objection to wood energy adoption.

"Too much work" was the main barrier or objection to wood energy adoption. This was most often cited in south-central Alaska (close to 45 percent of responses), and less often cited in the interior (close to 22 percent of responses). "Expensive" was rarely listed as an objection, especially among interior respondents. Also infrequently listed as a barrier was "not widely available yet." The interior appeared to have greatest overall availability of wood energy (i.e., least often cited "not widely available").

Most wood energy barriers (including "smoky," "expensive," "availability," and "too much work") were generally greatest for south-central respondents; therefore, it is not surprising that overall wood energy use was lowest in this region. There was great variation between regions in the "other" response (fig. 8). Here, respondents could write in any comment of their choice (either negative or positive).

Knowledge Regarding Residential Wood Burning

Most respondents were "somewhat" familiar with residential wood burning (fig. 9). South-central respondents had overall lower knowledge than those in southeast or interior Alaska, and southeast Alaska and interior Alaska respondents were fairly evenly matched across all knowledge levels. Once again, people more interested in wood energy may have been more likely to stop and complete a survey.

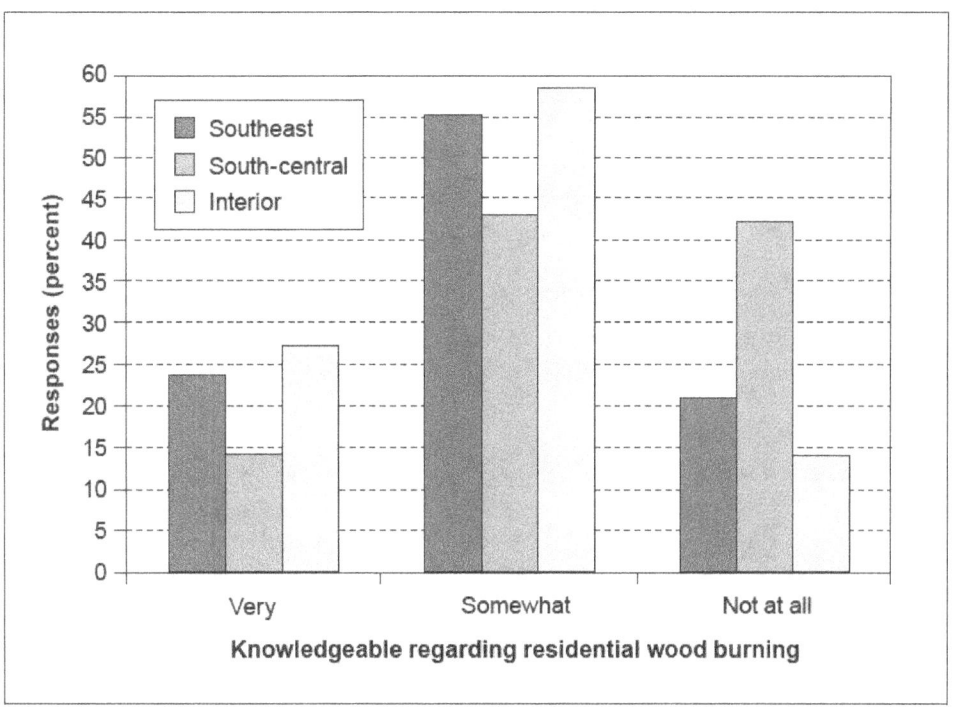

Figure 9—Knowledge level regarding residential wood burning, by Alaska region.

Knowledge Regarding Environmental Protection Agency Certified Woodstoves and Standards

Respondents were asked "How familiar are you with EPA certified woodstoves and/ or EPA standards for residential wood burning and air quality?" Most respondents were "not at all" familiar with Environmental Protection Agency (EPA) certified woodstoves (ranging from about 40 to 70 percent by region) (fig. 10). However, in interior Alaska this was fairly even between "somewhat" and "not at all" categories. South-central respondents had overall lower knowledge than southeast or interior Alaska, whereas interior respondents had overall greatest knowledge of EPA-certified woodstoves.

Environmental Protection Agency-certified woodstoves and other high-efficiency wood burners could help improve air quality within areas that are "at-risk." Juneau has experienced burn bans and other air quality issues in the Mendenhall Valley area. In Fairbanks, continued use of outdoor wood boilers could exacerbate winter air quality problems related to vehicle use. This could be significant given that Fairbanks is already an air quality nonattainment area for carbon monoxide (CO) and likely to be designated nonattainment for particulate matter (PM 2.5) as determined by the EPA (Alaska Division of Air Quality 2010).

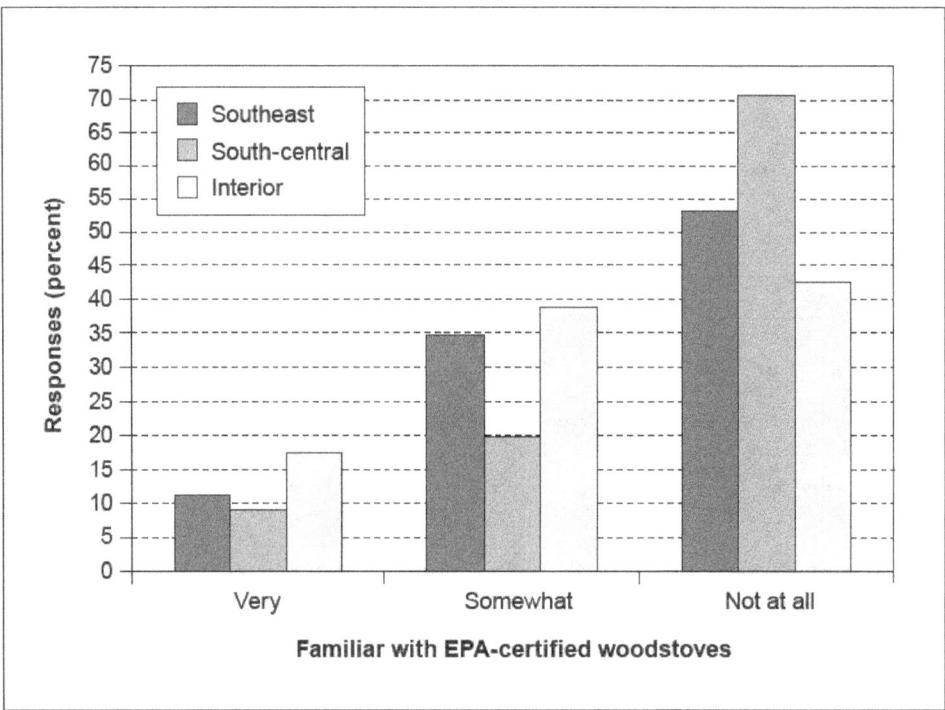

Figure 10—Familiarity with Environmental Protection Agency (EPA) certified woodstoves, by Alaska region.

Preferred Wood Fuel Types

Firewood/cordwood was by far the preferred wood fuel choice.

Firewood/cordwood was by far the preferred wood fuel choice, accounting for between 50 and 70 percent for responses for all regions (fig. 11). The interior had the highest preference for firewood (over 70 percent of respondents). Briquettes were least preferred with fewer than 10 percent of responses in all three regions (and 0 percent in the interior). South-central Alaska had a higher percentage of respondents answering "don't know" for preferred fuel type. The local wood fuel supply and availability could have influenced these responses (i.e., introduced a bias).

Wood Fuel Knowledge

Most respondents had either somewhat or very little overall knowledge of wood pellets (fig. 12). South-central respondents had the least overall knowledge of the three regions, and southeast and interior respondents were very closely matched for all three knowledge levels. Relatively few respondents considered themselves to be "very knowledgeable" regarding wood pellets. Most respondents had very little or no knowledge regarding wood briquettes (fig. 13), with between 75 and 85 percent of respondents, by region. Less than 5 percent of respondents in any region considered themselves "very familiar." Firewood was by far the type of wood fuel with

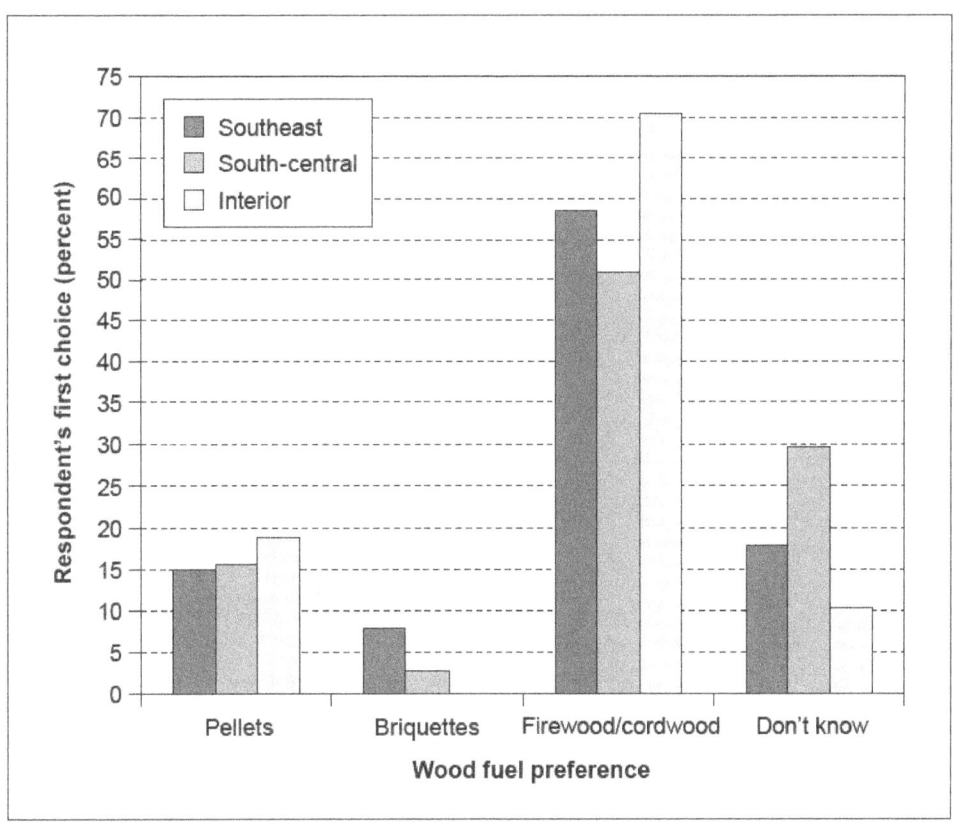

Figure 11—Preferred wood fuel types, by Alaska region.

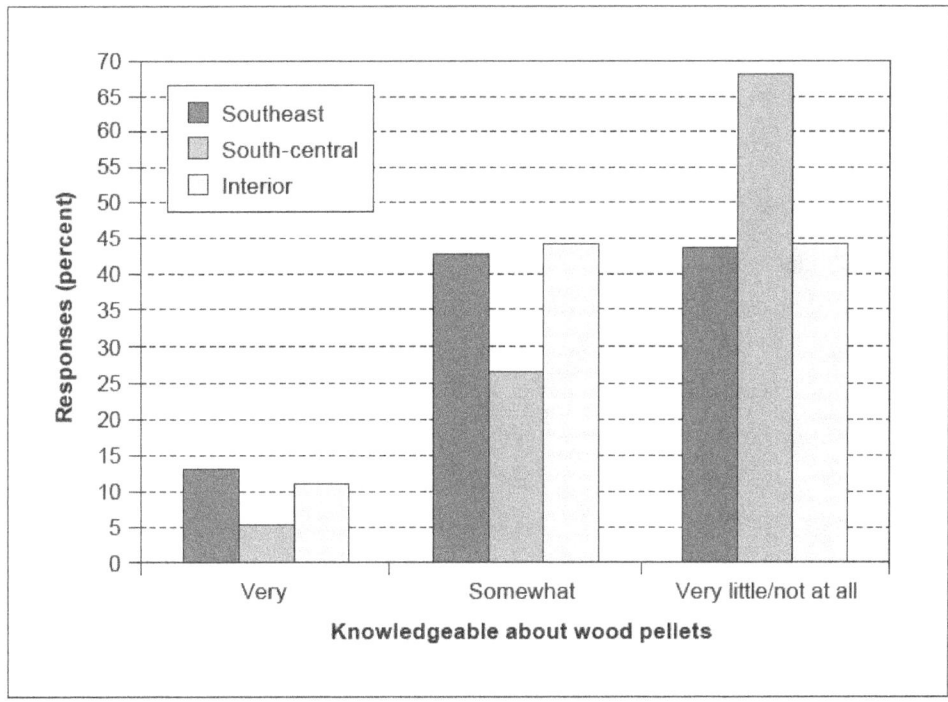

Figure 12—Knowledge level regarding wood pellet fuel, by Alaska region.

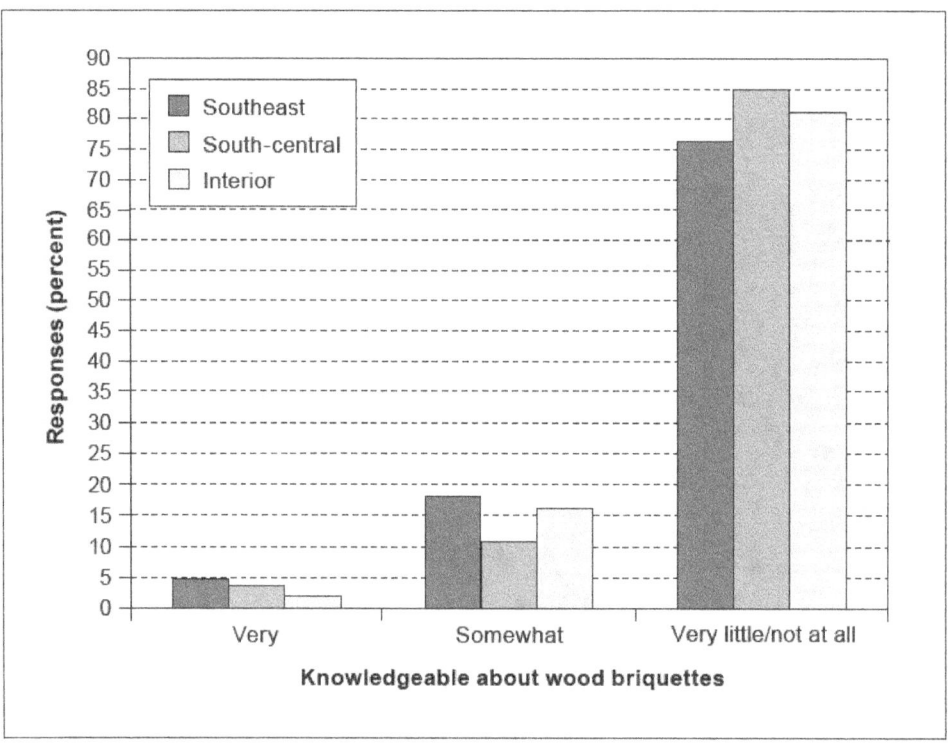

Figure 13—Knowledge level regarding wood briquette fuel, by Alaska region.

which respondents were most familiar (fig. 14). Overall, interior respondents had the greatest familiarity and south-central respondents the least familiarity. Similar to the results of "Preferred Wood Fuel Types," the local availability of the different types of wood fuel, as well as respondent experience with wood heating could have influenced these findings.

Fuel Oil Price Needed to Convert to Wood Energy

Most respondents indicated a price range of $4.00 to $5.00 per gallon as the market price for fuel oil at which they would convert to wood energy. Our results suggest that there is an "elbow" between $3.50 and $4.00 per gallon (fig. 15). At $3.50 per gallon fuel oil, very few people (about 5 percent of respondents at each location) were willing to switch to wood energy. Overall, a surprising number of respondents indicated that they would not switch from fossil fuels to wood heating, regardless of price. This was especially true among south-central respondents, where about 34 percent of respondents fit this category. This could be in part due to the relatively small sample size in Anchorage (n = 41), and because most respondents used natural gas and therefore did not respond to this question. Interior respondents indicated a sharp increase in willingness to convert between $4.00 and $5.00 per gallon (fig. 15).

Most respondents indicated a price range of $4.00 to $5.00 per gallon as the market price for fuel oil at which they would convert to wood energy.

18

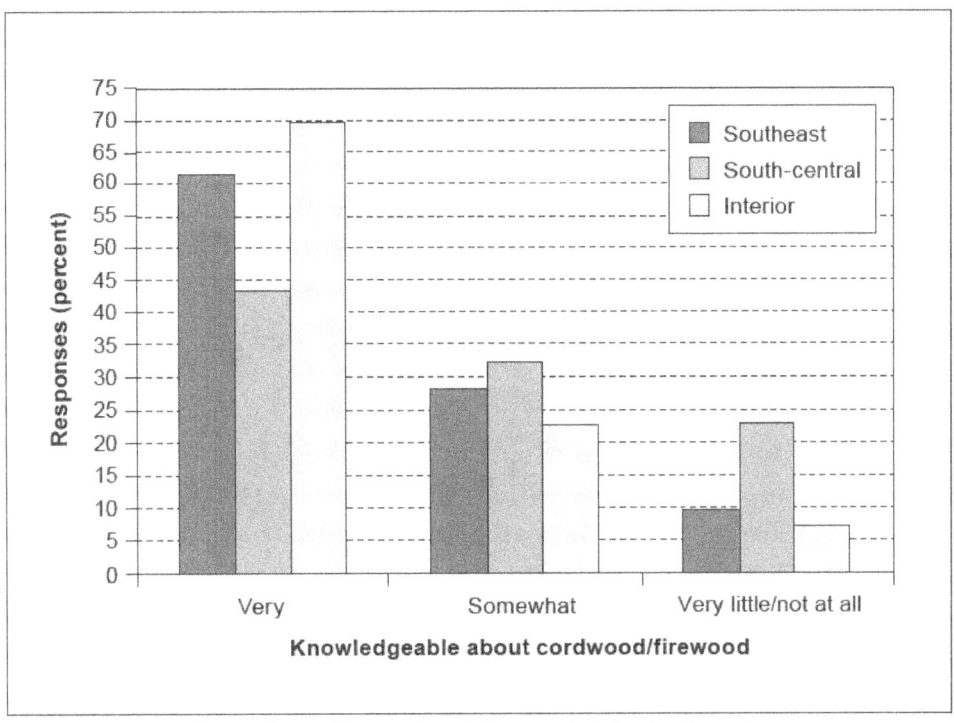

Figure 14—Knowledge level regarding cordwood/firewood fuel, by Alaska region.

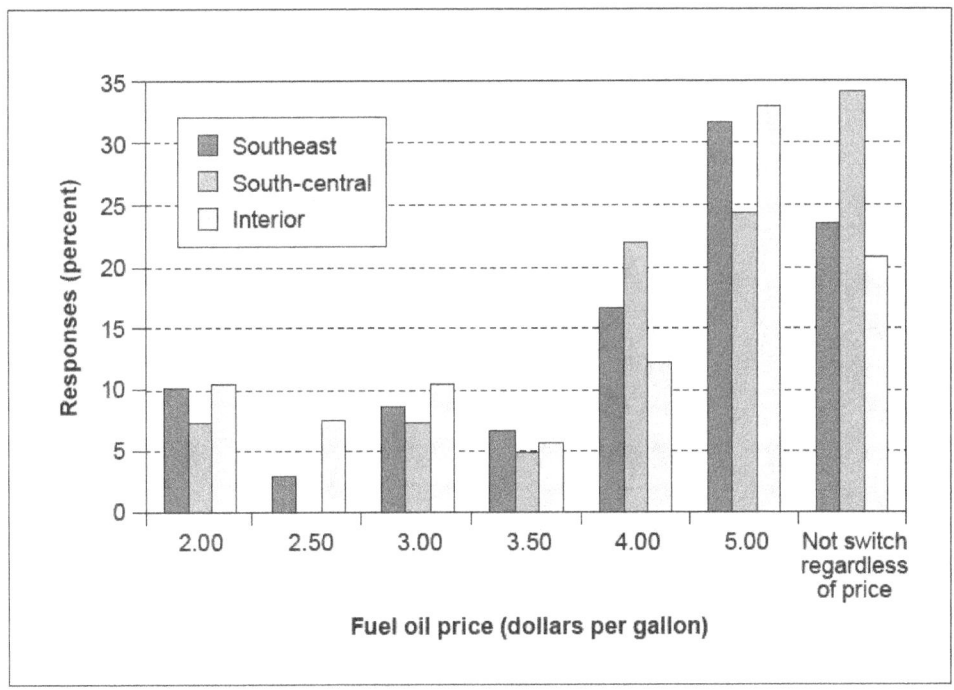

Figure 15—Fuel oil price needed to convert to wood energy, by Alaska region.

Note that fuel oil prices rose sharply during the data collection period (from about March to September 2008), and that interior respondents were sampled during the later part of this period, when fuel oil prices were higher. It is also likely that there was some variation in fuel oil market prices between regions, and in our study we did not attempt to normalize prices across sampling locations. Thus, fuel oil at a stated price may have seemed expensive to respondents in some locations, but not in other locations.

Maintenance Time Willing to Spend on Wood Energy System

Most respondents indicated a willingness to spend 15 to 30 minutes per day on maintenance for a residential wood energy system (fig. 16). Relatively few respondents indicated a willingness of 45 minutes per day or more maintenance time; however, the response rate was uniform between 45, 60, and more than 60 minutes per day. South-central Alaska had the highest proportion of respondents indicating "0 minutes per day" (approximately 20 percent of all respondents), and this was more than double that of southeast or interior. It is interesting to note that "too much work" was widely cited as a barrier to potential use of wood energy, also part of this same survey.

This question was presented hypothetically to respondents (i.e., they were asked "If you owned a wood energy system for home heating, how many minutes per day would you be willing to spend on maintenance?"). Therefore, the responses included prospective, as well as actual, wood energy users. Further, we defined

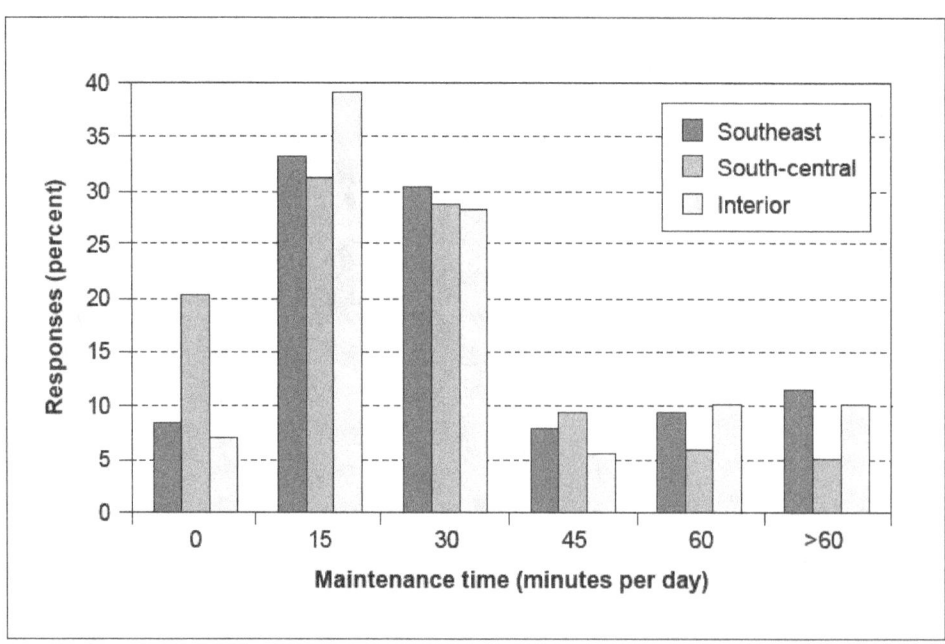

Figure 16—Maximum maintenance time willing to spend on wood energy system, by Alaska region.

"maintenance" to include a wide range of activities related to wood energy use, including receiving fuelwood (but not cutting or splitting it), "stoking" the burner, ash removal, and routine maintenance. Because our definition of "maintenance" was so broad, this could have influenced the higher proportion of respondents in the 45 minutes and greater categories.

Willingness to Pay for a Wood Energy System

Responses covered a broad range of prices; however, most respondents indicated a willingness to pay between $1,000 and $3,000. This would be within the price range of many commercial firewood and pellet home heating systems. South-central Alaska respondents had the greatest proportion of "$0" willingness to pay (about 22 percent of respondents) (fig. 17). For both southeast and interior Alaska, the highest response rate occurred for the $1,000 to $2,000 price range (with approximately 30 and 28 percent of respondents, respectively). A surprising number of respondents in the interior (approximately 14 percent) indicated a willingness to pay more than $5,000 for a new wood energy system.

Note that respondents included those who already owned wood energy systems as well as those who did not, and no information was provided to respondents about actual market prices for wood heating systems. Also, respondents' willingness to pay could have been influenced by their choice of wood energy system (e.g., firewood vs. wood pellets).

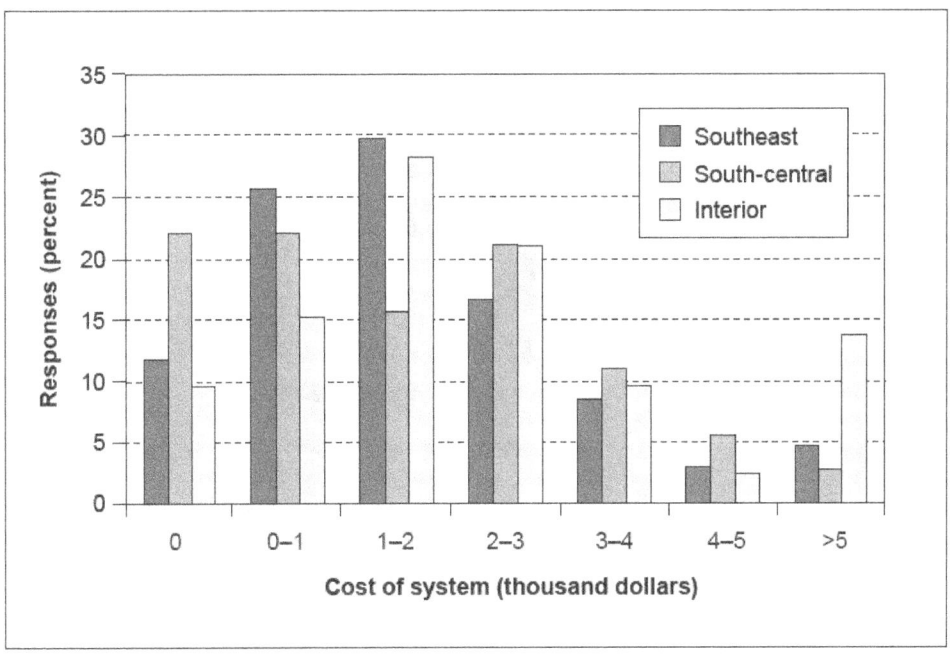

Figure 17—Amount willing to pay for new residential wood energy system, by Alaska region.

Willingness to Pay for Home Energy Efficiency

Respondents were asked how much they would be willing to pay annually for energy efficiency improvements to their home. Most responses ranged from $250 to $1,000 per year (fig. 18). Interior respondents indicated a high willingness to pay, with steadily increasing response rates from $0 per year to more than $1,000 per year. Indeed, the greatest response category was for interior residents at greater than $1,000 per year (almost 35 percent of respondents). About 60 percent of interior Alaska respondents indicated a willingness to pay $500 per year or greater. For southeast Alaska respondents, responses were fairly evenly distributed for all categories greater than $100 per year. Most south-central Alaska respondents indicated a willingness to pay $500 per year or less (almost 70 percent of respondents). A limitation of this question was that it asked for annual expenses for home energy efficiency. Based on feedback for those completing surveys, a more appropriate indicator might have been expenses over a longer period (perhaps 5 or 10 years), to more closely match actual spending habits for energy efficiency improvements.

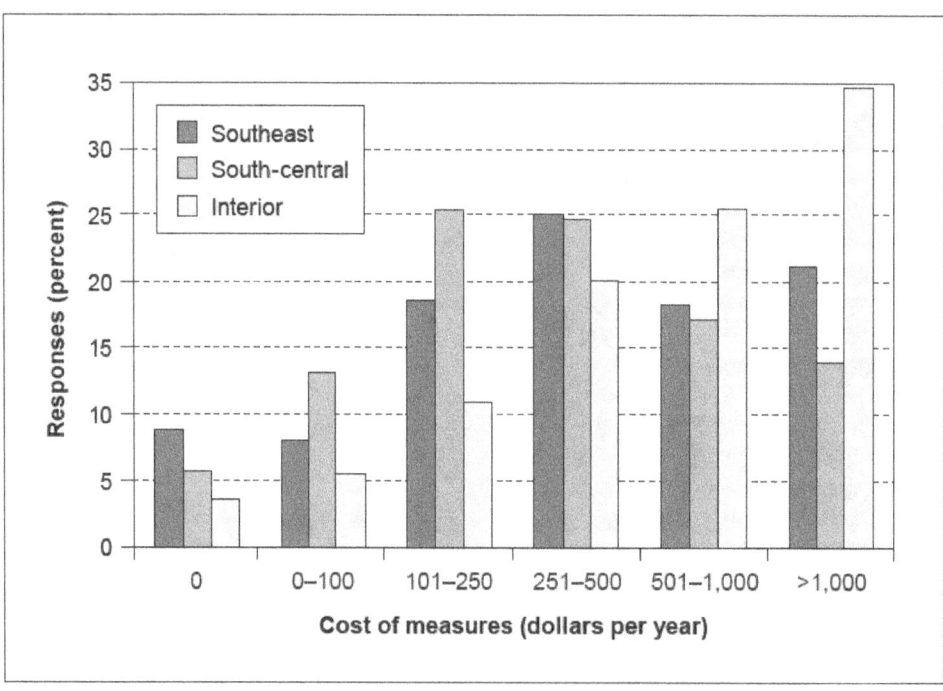

Figure 18—Willingness to pay for home energy efficiency measures, by Alaska region.

Conclusions

Current Conditions and Fuel Consumption

Current residential heating needs were met primarily by heating oil in southeast and interior Alaska, and by natural gas in south-central Alaska. Firewood was generally more important as a secondary fuel source (versus primary fuel source) in all regions of Alaska. Further, firewood was favored by a wide margin among wood fuel users in Alaska, with almost no current use of wood pellets, briquettes, or other densified fuel. This could be due to a lack of local sources for pellets, briquettes, or other densified fuel.

These results indicate that most Alaska households sampled have at least considered wood energy for home heating, and that the greatest near-term opportunity is for increased use of firewood. However, production of wood pellets and other densified fuels has been considered in Alaska, and the state's first major pellet facility is planned for operation in late 2009 (Mowry 2009). Separately, a pellet-making facility in Delta Junction, Alaska, has been in development for several years. Households that have multiple-fuel heating systems can increase their use of wood incrementally, as greater supplies become available. Although air quality issues were not considered in this paper, increased use of wood energy is likely to have some impact on emissions. This is an important concern in Alaska cities like Fairbanks and Juneau, where air quality can be a problem during winter months. Lastly, fuel oil price fluctuations could have an important influence on wood energy use and equipment purchasing decisions. Prices are currently well below recent highs, and it remains to be seen what impact this may have on wood energy use.

Knowledge and Attitudes

We found numerous regional variations in expected wood energy use between southeast, south-central, and interior Alaska. Cost was the most important factor influencing motivation to convert to wood energy. Of the three regions sampled, southeast Alaska respondents were the most concerned about finding local equipment vendors or local wood fuel suppliers. "Too much work" was the main barrier or objection to wood energy use for residential heating. Most respondents were at least somewhat familiar with residential wood burning, although Anchorage area respondents had overall lower knowledge than those in southeast or interior Alaska. Most respondents had very little familiarity with EPA-certified woodstoves. Firewood/cordwood was by far the preferred wood fuel choice, whereas compressed wood briquettes were least preferred. Similarly, knowledge of firewood was the highest of any fuel type.

These findings are significant because of the importance of consumer attitudes in influencing wood energy use and equipment purchasing decisions. As potential consumers become more knowledgeable about wood energy or adopt a favorable viewpoint, they will become more likely to use wood fuel. Outreach and education programs through schools, universities, and government agencies can have a beneficial effect in knowledge transfer and diffusion. Although these findings are important, they do not represent a random sampling of residents at the survey locations, and should not be used for marketing or product development decisions. The findings indicate the need for more detailed research on wood fuel use in Alaska, especially in regions of the state that were not sampled in this study.

Future Use and Conditions

We found numerous regional variations in expected wood energy use among southeast, south-central, and interior Alaska. This could be attributed to factors such as climate, familiarity with wood for home heating, and underlying preferences for nonwood fuel sources. We found that a fuel oil price of $4.00 to $5.00 per gallon should be sufficient to induce most homeowners to convert to wood heating. Although this fuel price (or higher) was prevalent in many parts of Alaska in summer 2008, recent dramatic price declines could already have an effect on consumer interest in wood energy. Most consumers were willing to pay from between $1,000 to $3,000 for new wood energy systems. However, the recent economic downtown (late 2008 and early 2009) could already have an influence on consumer spending decisions, their willingness to pay, and ability to borrow money. When considering expenses for home energy efficiency, most respondents were willing to pay between $250 and $1,000 per year, with interior residents at the higher end of this range. Fairbanks area residents also exhibited a greater willingness to pay for wood energy systems. Although household income was not evaluated in this study, it is an important consideration and could be incorporated into future research. This study identifies significant regional differences in the way Alaskans perceive wood energy, their potential use of wood for residential heating, and their willingness to pay for wood energy versus other sources.

Metric Equivalents

When you know:	Multiply by:	To find:
Acres	0.405	Hectares
Feet (ft)	.3048	Meters
Board feet, log scale	.0045	Cubic meters, logs
Board feet, lumber scale	.0024	Cubic meters, lumber
Tons	.907	Tonnes or Megagrams
Cords	3.625	Cubic meters
Gallons	3.78	Liters

Literature Cited

Alaska Division of Air Quality. 2010. Air non-point and mobile sources. http://www.dec.state.ak.us/air/anpms/pm/pm_fund.htm. (17 February 2010).

Barbour, R.J.; Zaborske, R.R.; McClellan, M.H.; Christian, L.; Golnick, D. 2005. Young-stand management options and their implications for wood quality and other values. Landscape and Urban Planning. 72: 79–94.

Bauman, M. 2005. Wood stove sales heat up as fuel prices skyrocket. Alaska Journal of Commerce. September 25. http://alaskajournal.com/stories/092505/hom_20050925016.shtml. (15 January 2009).

Brackley, A.; Crone, L. 2009. Estimating sawmill processing capacity for Tongass Timber: 2005 and 2006 update. Res. Note PNW-RN-561. Portland, OR: U.S. Department of Agriculture, Forest Service, Pacific Northwest Research Station. 15 p.

Brackley, A.M.; Parrent, D.J.; Rojas, T.D. 2006. Estimating sawmill processing capacity for Tongass timber: 2003 and 2004 update. Res. Note PNW-RN-553. Portland, OR: U.S. Department of Agriculture, Forest Service, Pacific Northwest Research Station. 18 p.

City and Borough of Sitka, Alaska. 2008. Resolution 2008-07. A resolution of the City and Borough of Sitka, Alaska supporting the development of a wood based fuel for space heating in Sitka. http://sitka.legistar.com/Legislation.aspx. (March 2010).

DeMars, D.J. 2000. Stand-density study of spruce-hemlock stands in southeastern Alaska. Gen. Tech. Rep. PNW-GTR-496. Portland, OR: U.S. Department of Agriculture, Forest Service, Pacific Northwest Research Station. 60 p.

Hanson, D. 2007. Analysis of wood volume available from hazard fuel reduction projects and development of wood residue markets in the Fairbanks area. Fairbanks, AK: State of Alaska, Department of Natural Resources, Division of Forestry. 23 p. http://forestry.alaska.gov/pdfs/07Biomass_Report.pdf. (15 January 2009).

Loy, W. 2009. Gas shortage stirs pols—governor, mayor, senator seek energy security as CI natural gas runs low. Petroleum News. Week of 9 August. http://www.petroleumnews.com/pntruncate/735566322.shtml. (17 February 2010).

Mowry, T. 2009. Wood pellet manufacturing plant planned for Fairbanks. Fairbanks Daily News-Miner. http://www.timberbuysell.com/community/DisplayAd.asp?id=4228. (March 2010).

Nicholls, D.L. 2009. Wood energy in Alaska—case study evaluations of selected facilities. Gen. Tech. Rep. PNW-GTR-793. Portland, OR: U.S. Department of Agriculture, Forest Service, Pacific Northwest Research Station. 33 p.

Nicholls, D.L.; Patterson, S.E.; Uloth, E. 2006. Wood and coal cofiring in interior Alaska: utilizing woody biomass from wildland defensible-space fire treatments and other sources. Res. Note PNW-RN-551. Portland, OR: U.S. Department of Agriculture, Forest Service, Pacific Northwest Research Station. 15 p.

Nowacki, G.; Shepard, M.; Krosse, P.; Pawuk, W.; Fisher, G.; Baichtal, J.; Brew, D.; Kissinger, E.; Brock, T. 2001. Ecological subsections of southeast Alaska and neighboring areas of Canada. Tech. Pub. No. R10-TP-75. Juneau, AK: U.S. Department of Agriculture, Forest Service, Alaska Region. 306 p.

Robb, S. 2007. Survey to assess community support for pellet fuel. Fairbanks, AK: Information Insights, Inc. Prepared for: Fairbanks Economic Development Corporation, 301 Cushman Street, Fairbanks, AK 99701. 36 p.

Tongass Futures Roundtable. 2008. Biomass energy. http://www.tongassfutures.net/biomass. (7 November 2009).

T.R. Miles Technical Consultants, Inc. 2006. Feasibility assessment for wood heating—final report. Prepared for Alaska Wood Energy Development Task Group. 80 p. http://jedc.org/forms/AWEDTG_WoodEnergyFeasibility.pdf. (6 May 2008).

U.S. Department of Agriculture, Forest Service [USDA FS]. 2007. Tongass National Forest, Prince of Wales Island, timber stand improvement. http://www.fs.fed.us/r10/tongass/districts/pow/projects_plans/timber/timber_stand_improv/young_growth.shtml. (4 February 2009).

U.S. Department of Agriculture, Forest Service [USDA FS]. 2008. Tongass National Forest land and resource management plan. R10-MB-603b. Juneau, AK: U.S. Department of Agriculture, Forest Service, Alaska Region. 468 p.

U.S. Department of Commerce, Bureau of Census [U.S. Census Bureau]. 2000. Census of housing—historical census of housing tables—house heating fuel. http://www.census.gov/hhes/www/housing/ census/historic/fuels.html. (20 March 2008).

Appendix

Questions asked of wood energy survey respondents:

Instructions and screening information
- Please answer the following questions regarding your use of fuels for home heating.
- Consider only space heating applications for your home (unless otherwise indicated).
- Please don't complete this survey if someone in your household has already responded.
- Please complete this survey only if you are a local resident.

Housing status
My housing status: ☐ I am a renter ☐   I am a home owner   ☐ I own 1 or more units that I rent out
    # of seasonal rental units: _____
    # of year-round rental units: _____

Survey questions
1. What is your primary heating source for your home?
    A. Heating oil
    B. Electricity
    C. Propane
    D. Firewood or cordwood
    E. Wood pellets
    F. Other wood source (specify) _____

2. What is your secondary heating source for your home?
    A. Heating oil
    B. Electricity
    C. Propane
    D. Firewood or cordwood
    E. Wood pellets
    F. Other wood source (specify) _____

3. What fuel does your hot water heater use? _____

4. Have you considered wood as a home heating source?
    Yes   or   No

5. If you have burned wood for home heating within the past year, please indicate the amount:
    # cords firewood _____   # tons pellets or briquettes _____

6. Have you purchased any wood burning equipment within the past 10 years?
    Yes   or   No

If yes, what type of equipment? _____

7. How familiar are you with EPA-certified woodstoves and/or EPA standards for residential wood burning and air quality?
    A. Very familiar
    B. Somewhat familiar
    C. Not at all familiar

8. Please indicate your fossil fuel used for home heating (if applicable)
   A. Primary fossil fuel used _____ (indicate type)
   B. Current fossil fuel market price (estimates OK) _____ ($ per gallon)
   C. Current fossil fuel consumption (estimates OK) _____ (gallons per year)

9. What factors might possibly motivate you to start using wood energy as a primary or secondary heating source for your home?
   A. If it costs less than fossil fuels, I'd consider it
   B. It's the environmentally responsible thing to do
   C. If there were local vendors for wood burning equipment in town, I'd consider it
   D. If there were local wood fuel suppliers, I'd consider it
   E. Other factors (please specify) _____

10. Which statements most closely characterize your viewpoint on wood energy for home heating?
    A. It's smoky
    B. It's expensive
    C. It's not widely available yet
    D. It's too much work to supply wood and/or maintain system
    E. Other _____

11. What is your level of knowledge regarding residential wood burning systems?
    A. Very knowledgeable
    B. Somewhat knowledgeable
    C. Not at all knowledgeable

12. When considering wood fuel, which would you prefer?
    A. Wood pellets
    B. Wood briquettes
    C. Firewood / cordwood
    D. Don't know

13. Please rate your knowledge on the following types of wood fuel:

Knowledge level	Wood pellets	Wood briquettes	Cordwood/firewood
Very knowledgeable			
Somewhat knowledgeable			
Very little or not at all knowledgeable			

14. How expensive would fuel oil need to become per gallon before you would consider converting to wood fuel? *(Please answer only if you are currently using fuel oil.)*
    A. $2
    B. $2.50
    C. $3
    D. $3.50
    E. $4
    F. $5
    G. I wouldn't switch, regardless of price

15. If you owned a wood energy system for home heating, how many minutes per day would you be willing to spend on maintenance? *(Please consider all related activities, including receiving fuelwood, "stoking" the burner, ash removal, maintenance, etc.)*
    A. 0 mins/day
    B. Up to 15 mins/day
    C. Up to 30 mins/day
    D. Up to 45 mins/day
    E. Up to 60 mins/day
    F. More than 60 mins/day

16. How much would you be willing to pay for a wood burning system?
    A. I would not consider paying anything
    B. $0–$1,000
    C. $1,001–$2,000
    D. $2,001–$3,000
    E. $3,001–$4,000
    F. $4,001–$5,000
    G. More than $5,000

17. How many square feet is your primary residence (approximate living space)? _____ (sq. ft.)

18. How many people live in your home? _____

19. Do you live in your local residence seasonally OR year-round?

20. How much would you be willing to pay per year to increase the energy efficiency of your home?
    A. Nothing ($0)
    B. $1–$100/year
    C. $101–$250/year
    D. $251–$500/year
    E. $501–$1,000/year
    F. More than $1,000/year

21. Please indicate your gender:
    A. Female
    B. Male

22. Please indicate your age:
    A. 18–30
    B. 31–40
    C. 41–50
    D. 51–60
    E. 61–70
    F. >70